UKULELE BASS

MW00582125

by **Martin Schroeder** and **Liselotte Schell**

Online Video

Video
dv.melbay.com/30058
You Tube
www.melbay.com/30058V

VIDEO CONTENTS

1 2 3 4 5 6 7 8 9 0

Visit us on the Web at www.melbay.com — E-mail us at email@melbay.com.

Introduction.

Congratulations! You have decided to buy an exciting new instrument: the bass ukulele. If you look at any group of instruments, the deepest sounding bass instrument is usually the biggest. The contrabass looks like a huge violin or the electric bass looks like a big guitar. By contrast, the original UBass is as small as a baritone ukulele, but is tuned to the same pitch as an upright or electric bass. This is as weird as a piccolo flute sounding like a tuba! Beneath this unique playing experience, the UBass offers a lot of advantages. You can look forward to easy and relaxed playability as well as the light weight of this tiny instrument. A built-in pickup system also provides the UBass with a massive sound so that 'the little one' can keep up on stage.

This book contains an introduction to the bass ukulele as well as to its development, history, handling, care and maintenance. We will also answer the most interesting question: 'where does that deep, massive sound come from?' Co-author Martin 'Bassmati' Schroeder examined the UBass in rehearsal, on stage and in the studio and gives us his impressions and experiences.

The last part of this book offers easy exercises for the bass ukulele as well as easy, catchy grooves. True to the motto 'great minds think alike' we brought bass ukulele and cajon (a boxed-shaped percussion instrument) together and show you how a real rhythm section grooves!

I want to thank all the people that made this international edition work. Thanks to my Co-author Martin "Bassmati" Schroeder, Felix Schell, Max Schneider, Gabriele Kurth-Schell, John Taylor and Stacey Kight.

Many Thanks to Rick Carlson and the whole Kala Team for their support, as well as to Rigk Sauer (RISA Musical Instruments). Last but not least – many thanks to Collin Bay for releasing this issue in record time.

Now, let's start! Enjoy the UBass!

Liselotte Schell

Content.

The bass ukulele.

'More bass, less space' - this is the best description of this new bass instrument, its powerful sound and portable size. Compared to the ratio of the cajon to the actual drum set, the bass ukulele offers the bass player a small but massive sounding instrument whose sound is something between an electric and an upright bass. Despite its short scale, the bass ukulele manages to keep up with its big brothers on stage as well as in the studio. The special sound of the bass ukulele makes it the perfect accompanying instrument for the folk and country styles.

The bass ukulele is a convenient, value for money bass with a massive sound right between the sound of an electric and an upright bass. It is a useful extension of equipment for the modern bass player as well as a great opportunity for beginners or other instrumenalists to learn the most powerful instrument: the bass!

Tuning your UBass.

At a 21" scale, the "Little Monster" is hardly bigger than a baritone ukelele but leads to enormous surprise from the audience. The bass player, who is usually lurking at the back of the stage, becomes the center of attention. The sound produced by this amplified bass ukulele is simply amazing. The secret of the bass ukulele tone lies in its polyurethane strings in conjunction with its size (20 inch scale length) and a pickup system that creates a sound that is both traditional and progressive. The bass ukulele is tuned to standard bass tuning of E-A-D-G.

Development of Kala UBass models.

The first UBass models were developed by Owen Holt of Road Toad Music. For his private customers he manufactured bass ukuleles in single-unit production. When his waiting list grew, he collaborated with Mike Upton, President of Kala, and brought the first UBass to the market through Kala Brand Music Co. The original Kala UBass was based on the "Road Toad Big Bufo Bass" and modelled after the baritone ukulele in both size and body. Before then, the Baritone Ukulele had always been the Uke with the deepest sound on the planet. The baritone ukulele is tuned to D-G-B-E, which corresponds to the four highest strings of a guitar in standard tuning. The "Big Bufo Bass" was built around the use of nylon strings, which sounded deep, but always one octave higher than an average electric or upright bass. Owen developed special strings to give the small bass ukulele its upright bass sound, but more on those later...

Kala UBASS - fretted version

The UBass manufacturer Kala is offering different „UBass"-models for purchase. The first Kala UBass was released in 2009. In spring 2010, Kala released the "UBass 2" Series, which is available in fretted and fretless versions and provides an affordable alternative to the original UBass whilst maintaining all the features and functionality. "Fretless" is a term for instruments, that do not have frets on the neck, just like a violin or an upright bass. To make the finding of the right fingering easier, Kala applied inlaid fret lines for a better orientation while playing. The UBass can be obtained in spruce, acacia or mahagony variation, fretted or fretless. The scale measures 51cm with 16 frets.

The Scale is the sounding length of the strings of an instrument, which is measured between the inside of the nut to the center of the bridge saddle. Each UBass is equipped with a passive pickup system with 4 individual piezo elements that together provide a balanced and powerful sound.

In the meantime, Kala offers several UBass models in a solid body version. They are available in fretted or fretless versions, in 4 or 5 string models. The expression "solid body" describes instruments that do not contain a soundbox, unlike acoustic instruments, but largely consist of solid wood. These UBass models are manufactured in the US and are part of the Kala "California Series".

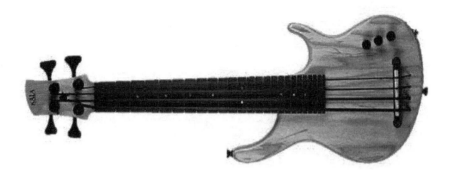

One of Kala's UBass Solid Body models.

In 2011, Kala introduced the new S-U-B (Subductive) imported solid body - series as an affordable alternative to the "California Series" of solid body basses. The bass instruments of the "S-U-B series" are also available in 4- and 5-string models. The Name of the subductive UBass model is, like the Pahoehoe Strings, inspired by a natural phenomenon. Subduction is a geological term used to describe how, for instance, the Mariana Trench, the deepest known point in the Pacific Ocean, was created. The SUB-Models come with a shadow pickup system with volume control. Kala has recently (at the time of publication of this book) announced five new UBass Models on NAMM 2012, e.g. a Hutch Hutchinson signature model as well as several new colours "sunburst", "gloss black", "spalted maple" and "exotic mahogony".

To keep up with the latest developments we recommend a visit on Kala's site (www.kalaukulele.com) or on the UBass blogs, "UBass Appreciation Society" (http://ubassappreciation.wordpress.com) and "Play UBass" (http://playubass.com).

Kala UBASS solid body S-U-B series.

Bass Ukulele Manufacturers.

Besides Kala, other manufacturers are offering bass ukulele models, such as Stevens and Ortega. Manufacturer Stevens released their bass ukulele-model during the music trade fair in Frankfurt 2011. The instrument is manufactured out of cedar and Sitka spruce wood, bottom and rib out of rosewood. Particularly noteworthy are the strings, which Stevens developed in collaboration with the string manufacturer Pyramid. These strings are built like classical guitar strings, but have a core of nylon fibers tightly bound by wire coated in silver. The effect, according to the manufacturer, is a string that, despite its huge diameter, is flexible enough to produce an opulent and harmonic sound.

The secret of the bass ukulele: "Pahoehoe Strings".

The secret behind the deep sound of this small instrument is in the stringing. The Kala UBass models are equipped with polyurethane strings, designed by Owen Holt of Road Toad Music. These polyurethane strings (Pahoehoe strings) have a higher mass than nylon strings and lead to a great duplication of an upright bass sound. When tuned, the string diameters range from .070" to .185".

Polyurethane, the material used for the strings, is any polymer composed of a chain of organic units joined by urethane links. It was synthesized 1937 by Otto Bayer and his coworkers. These synthetic materials and resin can be found in several forms, e.g. expanding foam, gumboots, bowling balls, soccer balls, lacquer or even dish mops.

The term "Pahoehoe" refers to the black ropey lava that forms from the flows of the active volcanoes of Hawaii. Pahoehoe-Strings are available in diverse colors (standard: black, colored: yellow, red, green) and different tensions to fit the respective playing style. For the Kala UBass, the regular tension strings are recommended.

Standard set:	Low tension set:	Long scale set:
E .200"	E .236"	E .187"
A .187"	A .197"	A .162"
D .156"	D .139"	D .139"
G .125"	G .118"	G .118"

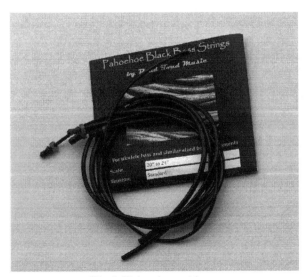

Black Pahoehoe strings.

Maintenance of strings.

New Pahoehoe strings will go through a short period of stretching until they arrive at their final state. This cannot be compared to normal tuning of normal guitar strings. The process can be expedited by gently tugging on the strings, then tuning the strings to pitch several times until the strings no longer drop in pitch. And a word to the wise! Be sure to have only two or three wraps around the tuning head, otherwise the maintenance of the strings could be affected in a negative way. If you count more than three wraps around the mechanic, you should consider unwrapping and retuning the string with fewer wraps.

And remember – its plastic! Always keep your strings clean to keep your UBass grooving.

"Thundergut" strings.

As an alternative to the Pahoehoe strings, the Italian string manufacturer Aquila offers "Thundergut" strings for the bass ukulele. According to Aquila, "Thundergut" is "a special very dense and elastic plastic blend" which was developed in the Aquila headquarters. The manufacturer claims in his advertisement that his blend provides a better performance compared to common polyurethane and silicon rubber strings. In addition, the Aquila strings would "insure a quick and stable intonation" without the typical stretching process during tuning. Unlike silicone rubber strings, the surface of the strings would be "less sticky and slippery" when touched.

Every bass player should try the different strings to find your preferred stringing.

As mentioned above, string manufacturer Pyramid also developed special bass ukulele strings in cooperation with Stevens Guitars (nylon-wrapped).

Aquila's white Thundergut strings

The bass ukulele - Live!

Since the introduction of the first Kala UBass in 2009, the UBass has found its way into studios and live performances and in the hands of many notable artists that include Bakithi Kumalo (Paul Simon), Hector Maldonado (Train), Jim Mayer (Jimmy Buffett), and Reggie McBride (Keb Mo). It has also been featured in the popularTV series, "Glee" and the film "Just Go With It". In Germany the bass ukulele has been seen in the live performances of famous artists, such as Udo Lindenberg, Annett Louisan and Xavier Naidoo.

Kala Endorser Hutch Hutchinson (e.g. Bonnie Raitt) to whom the signature model was devoted said: "The Kala Solid Body U-Bass is a true innovation in the world of bass, - really fun to play, sounds great live or in the studio, and is extremely portable." Other endorsees are Tal Wilkenfeld (Jeff Beck, Herbie Hancock), Abraham Laboriel, Stuart Hamm and Esperanza Spalding.

Bakithi Kumalo (Paul Simon), Kala Endorser:

"This Little Monster is the Future of Bass, and it's here"

Reggie McBride (Keb Mo, Rickie Lee Jones), Kala Endorser:

"This bass has more bottom end than any bass I own."

The parts of your UBass.

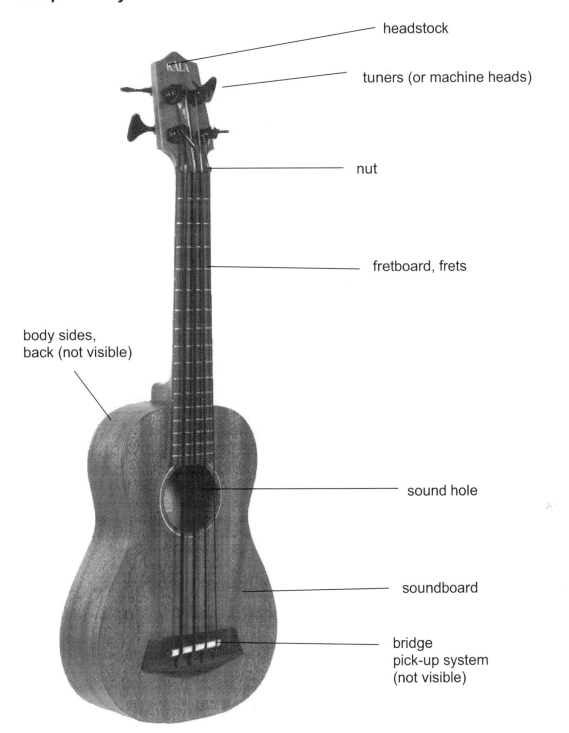

headstock

tuners (or machine heads)

nut

fretboard, frets

body sides,
back (not visible)

sound hole

soundboard

bridge
pick-up system
(not visible)

The scale.

The scale, which is also called string length or string measure is defined as the maximum vibrating length of the stings to produce sound and determines the range of tones that the strings are capable to produce under a given tension. It is measured between the inside of the nut to the center of the bridge saddle.

The octave.

The octave is an interval (an interval is a gap between two notes) with eight whole tone steps within one musical pitch, and another with half or double its frequency. 'Okta' is Latin for the number eight.

Scale and octave.

The octave of every open string can be found on the 12th fret of the Instrument. This octave-point is found right in the middle of the scale, often at the transition of neck to body of the instrument.

scale „S"

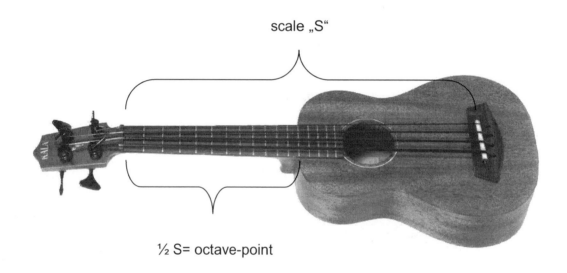

½ S= octave-point

The octave is usually marked with two dots and can be usually find directly on the transition from the neck to the body of the instrument.

Tune you bass ukulele.

Track 01

The Tuning.

The UBass has to be tuned accurately before playing. Thanks to the Pahoehoe Strings made out of Polyurethane, your UBass can be tuned in standard bass tuning to E, A, D, G. To tune your instrument correctly, you can choose one of the following alternatives.

Tuning with a tuner.

Most bassists or guitar players use an electronic tuner to tune their instrument. The tuner most commonly displays a red or green light if the plucked string is in tune or not. Tuners are available quite cheap and there is a wide variety of different models. To find a suitable tuner for your bass ukulele, please contact your local dealer. We recommend you use a tuner for your UBass. The Polyurethane stings go through a long stretching process and they are quite difficult to tune correctly once you are on stage or in the studio. A good tuner in indispensable!

Tuning by ear.

The ambitious player will insist on tuning the bass ukulele by ear. This tuning method requires a point of reference at first (a tuning fork or your piano). If your second string (A-string) tuned correctly, the other strings get their tone by comparison. The respective tone for comparison can be found on the 5th fret of the string above.

A - string (5th fret)= D

D - string (5th fret) = G

The pitch of the E - string can be found by tapping the 2nd fret of the D-string. This is an octave comparison.

Track 02

Tuning with harmonics.

Natural harmonics or 'flageolets' can be found above or on the 5th, 7th and 12th fret. Create the flageolet sound by putting your first finger very gently on the string right above the fret. Do not tap. When you strike the string, take your first finger away from the string immediately. You will recognize the harmonics by their high and clear sound. For tuning your UBass by harmonics, compare the flageolet on the 5th fret with the sound of the flageolet on the 7th fret of the sting below. Please have a look at Track 02 of our video for a detailed example.

Stretching and dwindling tension.

New polyurethane strings will go through a massive stretching process. It will take a while until the stretching is over and the strings will keep their tune and tension. Please avoid a layering of the stings on the mechanical heads. The strings will get brittle if you layer them as the material is very sensitive.

Playing posture.

The bass ukulele can be played seated as well as standing up. If you choose a standing posture, a strap is recommended to make sure that you play your bass in a relaxed position. Without a strap, your right arm is responsible for keeping the instrument in place. The common posture is seated whilst placing the instrument on your right knee. In this position you have great mobility in both hands to reach every fret. This posture is preferred by many players and considered the most comfortable.

Common playing posture on left knee.

Relaxed playing posture on right knee.

Standing playing posture.

Fundamentals.

Left and right hand.

Here we differentiate between the tapping and the strumming hand. The fingers of the tapping hand are marked with the numbers 1 to 4, the finger of your strumming or plucking hand are marked with the letters p (thumb), i, m and a (pointer, second and third finger).

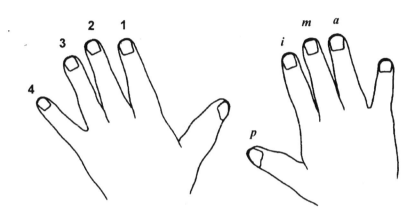

Fingering.

An accurate fingering helps to play smoothly and fluently. But how do you know where to put your fingers in correct fingering? The fingering offers rules that you should consider. Basically, the fingering depends on the playing position.

Basic Fingering.

Put your fingers 1,2,3 and 4 one after another on fret 1-4 along one string (in a chromatic order). We start with finger 1 tapping the first fret of the deepest string, Finger 2 on the second fret of the deepest E-String Finger 3 on the third fret and so on. Continue with the other strings. In position II, we start with Finger 1 on the second fret and continue as described above. In Position III we start with finger 1 on the third fret.

Watch out for fingering directions in your sheet music!

Playing methods.

Here we differentiate between different plucking methods. You can pluck with your thumb, pluck in alternate picking or pluck the string with a plectrum. A plectrum is a small, flat piece of plastic that is used to pluck or strum guitar strings. Plectrums, also called 'picks', are available in different strengths and sizes and most commonly triangle shaped. Pulling the string with your thumb offers the advantage that you can use the heel of your hand to mute the strings. Alternate picking is done by the pointer and second finger of your right hand with your thumb placed on the thickest string or above. The strings are pulled alternately by first and second finger. Every playing method offers advantages. Advanced players vary their playing methods to suit the song.

Play with a plectrum ("pick").

Play in alternate picking.

Pull with your thumb.

Before you start to play.

Notes and TAB.

Besides notes, tones are displayed by a system called tablature or 'TAB' for short. Every notation in this book is equipped with common notation and notation in TAB. The TAB notation shows the tapped fret and the string to pluck. Beware: even if you do not like to learn the common notation, you have to understand it to some extend. This is important to understand the rhythm.

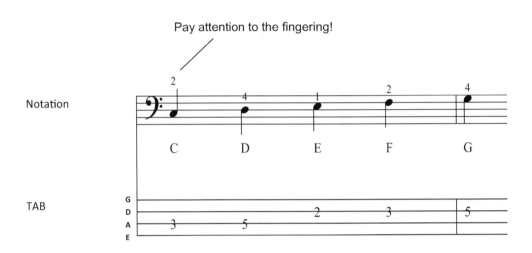

Beneath the common notation, you can see the TAB notation with four lines that match the four strings of your UBass. The deepest sounding string, the E-string can be found on the bottom. The example above shows the following sounds: 3rd and 5th fret on the A-string, 2nd, 3rd and 5th fret of the D-string.

Exercise 1.

Play the exercise below in every playing method (thumb, pick and alternate picking).

Exercise 2.

Play the following piece in all playing methods. If you take a look at the video, you can clearly recognize the difference between staccato (short, tense) and legato (swings).

BOOGIE-WOOGIE

Track 03—08

Interview with Martin 'Bassmati' Schroeder, co-author, multi-instrumentalist and professional bass player.

We asked Martin if he could highlight some characteristics and features of the UBass. Martin plays a UBass model of the Kala UBass 2 Series with a sprouce top and Pahoehoe Strings.

Martin, you work as a bass teacher in several music schools around Hamburg, Gemany. What would you recommend to someone who just bought a UBass as his first or second instrument to learn?

If I'm teaching a new student who just bought a UBass, the first thing I check is that they cut their fingernails. This is very important because the black thick strings of the bass are very sensitive and pick up scratches very easily. Long fingernails prevent a proper playing style and you can't get the right tone.

Which playing style do you recommend for the UBass?

To an adult beginner, I would always recommend to start with alternate picking right away. To play in alternate picking I rest the thumb of my right hand on the first string (E-String) and strike the other strings alternately with first and second finger. If the beginner is a child, I would start with plucking the strings with the thumb. Advanced players mute the strings with the heel of their right hand to get a softer sound. Of course you can also play with a pick. If you compare the sound of your UBass in alternate picking and playing with a pick you'll hear the difference. Alternate picking is very adjustable and leads to a typical, warm and soft bass sound. If you pluck the strings with a pick you'll get a tough sound. The UBass also offers the limited possibility to play chords by plucking the strings.

Are there any other typical characteristics, especially with playing posture?

You can play your UBass like a guitar, either on the right or on your left knee. If you play on the left knee – just like a classical guitar - you have the bass quite near to your body. This way you have a really good overview what is happening on the small-fretted neck of your Ubass while playing. If you choose to place your bass on the right knee, it is further away from your body, easier to play and the whole thing just looks cooler to me *(laughs)*.

What do you think of the Polyurethane Strings?

Oh, I will always have difficulties remembering this technical term but I will not forget these strings in a hurry. At the moment, my bass is equipped with black Pahoehoe strings. The strings are thick and floppy and very elastic. They feel just like a clothsline. This feature demands very cautious handling – with a normal electic bass you will feel a completely different tension. That's why you should hold back a little while playing. If you pluck too hard, the sound gets warped very easily. This Bass really requires a smooth, sensitive playing style. The tuning of the strings is not easy and you need to do a lot of stretching. I would highly recommend a good tuner.

The UBass is not only an acoustic instrument, is it?

That's right. Beneath the bridge of the UBass, you can find the built-in pickup system. On the back of my bass, there is a small hatch, which you can lift up ad see the piezo pick-up inside. This pickup is used with other acoustic instruments too, such as cello or violin. The pick-up of my UBass is responding quite fast and hard, you can try to hear the response of your pick-up by tapping carefully with your thumb around the bridge of your UBass.

You just came out of the studio where you recorded with the newcomer artist Tom Klose. Did you take your UBass with you and can you tell about specialities of the instrument in the studio?

Yes, that's right, we just finished the recordings. For sure, I took my UBass with me and recorded bass lines for several track with it. Due to the thickness of the strings, the short scale and the specific sound of the UBass several advantages and disadvantages occurred during the recordings. I utilized the UBass for "folky" pop songs. If you listen to the sound of the UBass very carefully you will recognize that the tone is very similar to the sound of an upright bass. It is very short and decays very fast. This sound is perfect for folk, country or western songs that ask for a short and upright bass—style bass line. That's great in the recording too. If you require resonance and length in the bass sound, I would always use an electric bass.

How does the audience react to the UBass?

The UBass goes down very well with the crowd. The UBass really gets a lot of attention on stage. The crowd goes wild seeing a tall man like me charming deep tones out of a small ukelele.

What would you recommend to a beginner?

The UBass is very easy to play and good for beginners. If you just started, you should start with plucking every single string with your thumb and listen to the tone very carefully. As you go along you have to feel and recognize how to tap the strings with your left hand the best way and to pluck with the right to get a good tone. The strings are very thick, the frets very small. If you tap too weak, or in the wrong spot on the fret you will not get a proper tone out of your bass – if you press too hard the note goes out of tune. After you've got that, you can start with easy tunes.

Anything to add – any closing advice?

Indeed! Please don't slap your UBass. Slapping should be avoided – the UBass is definitely not built for that playing style.

I'm confident that the UBass will continue its triumph to gain a strong position in suitable playing genres. (Singer-Songwriter, Country, Folk, Pop, Soul, Hip Hop and so on) The little monster can nearly replace its bigger brother the upright bass, is easier to learn and more mobile, that's for sure!

Go UBass go!!

Range and fret board.

The UBass's range is two and a half octaves. From the deepest sounding tone (E – open string) we go to middle A (14th fret – G-string) and beyond.

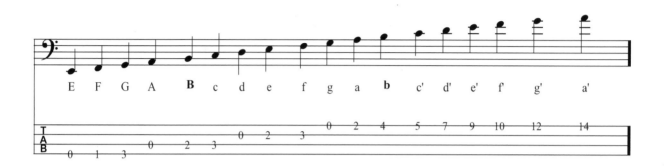

Identical tones.

There is a huge number of sounds that you can find on your fret board several times. These 'identical tones' can be found on every stringed instrument, for example guitar, mandolin, banjo or violin. While playing, you can always find different methods of interpreting the song on your fret board. As a bass player, it is your job to find the best method for you. The choice depends on the sound and playability.

If you use tablature you have to accept the choice of the arranger.

Examples of identical tones.

Basics of music theory.

Whole tone Steps – half tone steps.

The diatonic scale, c,d,e,f,g,a and b consists of whole- and half tone steps. You can find the half stepps between e and f as well as between b and c. Half steps can always be found right on the next fret. There is no fret in between.

Whole tone steps are reached by skipping one fret. The fret in between is left open.

Accidentals and key signature.

Chromatic signs or 'accidentals' are special signs that have an effect on the pitch of the notes. A sharp raises and a flat lowers the pitch of a note one semitone while a natural is used to cancel this effect. If accidentals are placed right at the beginning of the stave right next to the clef, the accidentals affect the entire piece. This is called the 'key signature'.

Modes.

There are 12 different modes. Every composition can be transposed in different modes. With the transponation, the only thing that changes ist he pitch.

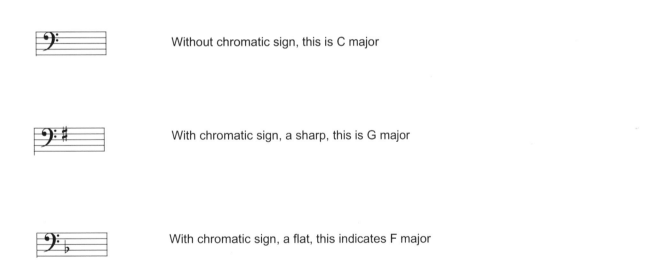

Without chromatic sign, this is C major

With chromatic sign, a sharp, this is G major

With chromatic sign, a flat, this indicates F major

Accidentals.

In contrast to the key signature that affects the entire piece, accidentals affect single tone pitches within the composition. They raise or lower the following note from its normal pitch. The symbols used to mark such accidentals are sharps and flats. A natural relieves the effect of the accidental. If you find a sharp right next to a notehead, the note is raised by a semitone (e.g. from F to F sharp).

To make a semitone interval just move your tapping finger from your left hand one fret along the neck. With flats, it's just the other way round.

Sign for a sharp: ♯

Sign for a flat: ♭

Sign for a natural: ♮

Validity of accidentals.

An accidental is valid for the whole bar. If it is meant to be valid only for one note, you will find a natural right next to the next identical tone.

Example with sharps and flats:

A half tone step up with a sharp.

A half tone step down with a flat.

Example with a natural:

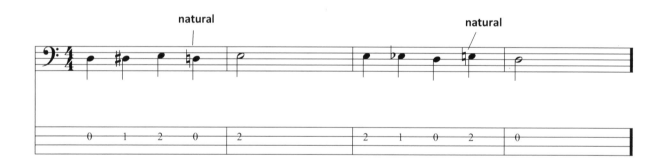

Rhythm and Measure.

Introduction.

The bass player is part of the rhythm section which consists of drums, bass and piano and sometimes guitar. The rhythm section is responsible for the 'drive' of the band. An experienced rythm section is the ideal background for every soloist.

Rythm notation.

The rhythm notation alters the appearance of single notes in a piece. It defines the relative duration that these notes occupy within the composition.

Axis of time ————————————

Example 1: Walk and count your footsteps. Try to stress the 'one' a little: **1**,2,**1**,2,**1**,2,**1**,2..... try to stay at the same speed.

Example 2: Walk and count your footsteps : **1**,2,3,**1**,2,3,**1**,2,3,**1**,2,3.....

Example 3: Walk and count your footsteps : **1**,2,3,4,**1**,2,3,4,**1**,2,3,4,**1**,2,3,4.....

Measure.

Beats are grouped into bars or 'measures' as they are also called. In our examples before, at first 2, then 3 and last but not least 4 beats were grouped into one bar.

Example 4:

Repeat examples 1-3 and imagine you were 'walking through' the piece with this beat. Bar lines are placed just before every '1'.

How did you react? Did you apply a little break at the bar line or did you move on constantly? Bar lines divide the piece into bars but do not have an effect on the speed.

Example 5:

Extend examples 1-3 by clapping your hands with every footstep. Your footsteps define the beat, the clapping relates to a rhythmic event. At first these two happen simultaneously.
The note value tells you when to play the note and how long to hold it. A rest value tells you when and for how long not to play anything.

Whole note.
The whole note lasts for 4 beats and fills up a bar in which 4 beats are grouped.

Half note.
The half note lasts for 2 beats (it is half of a whole note). In comparison to the whole note, a stem is added. Two half notes fill up a bar with 4 beats.

Quarter note.
Quarter notes last for 1 beat. That means that four quarter notes fit into one 4/4 bar.

Rhythm exercises.

Clap the following exercises and tap the beat with your foot. If you are not sure how to do it, have a look at our video.

Track 09

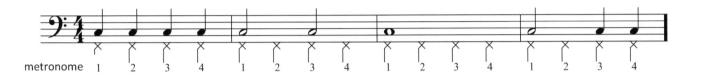

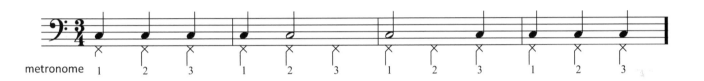

The metronome.

There are electronic and mechanic metronomes available. The metronome sets the beat. If you use your metronome regularly, your timing will improve.

Timing.

Timing means the adherence to a set tempo. It is important to keep the pace.

Beats per minute.

The different tempi are measured in beats per minute (bpm). If a tempo of 60 is indicated, a quarternote lasts for a second (this tempo is rather slow). The speed 120 indicates exactly two quarter notes per second. Like this, a clock can be used as metronome.

Tempo indication.

Largo (40 - 52 beats per minute)

Adagio (54 - 60)

Andante (63 - 76)

Moderato (80 - 96)

Allegro (100 - 138)

Presto (144 - 176)

Prestissimo (184 - 208)

Rests.

For every note value there is corresponding rest values such as a 'whole rest' which also lasts for four beats. The whole rest instructs you not to play your UBass for four beats. The half rest lasts for two beats and the quarter rest lasts for 1 beat.

whole rest   half rest   quarter rest

whole note   half note   quarter note

Counting in.

To indicate the tempo of a piece, musicians count in. Usually two bars are counted in.

Now count: 'one –two –one, two, three, four'

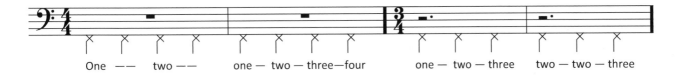

Pickup.

A pickup, also called anacrusis is a sequence of notes or only one note which precedes the first down-beat in a bar. Most commonly, the anacrusis is only played by one instrument of the band. It is counted in one-two-one.

Eight note and dotted quarter note.

An eight note lasts for half a beat and looks just like a quarter note but with a flag attached to the stem.

Many basslines contain dotted quarter notes. The dot behind the notehead of a quarter note increases the duration of the quarter by half of its original length. Thus the dotted quarter is a normal quarter plus an eight note and lasts for one and a half beats.

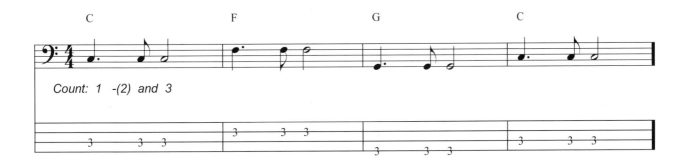

Scales in first position.

Pay attention to the fingering.

Track 10

G major scale

Track 11

F major scale

Track 12

A major scale

Track 13

E major scale

C-major – second position.

Pay attention to the fingering!

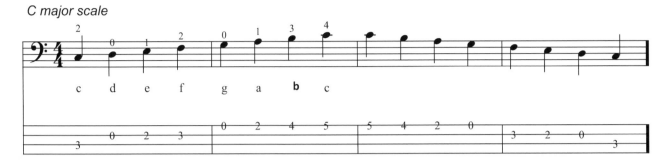

D major scale – position change.

First position with a change to the 6th position.

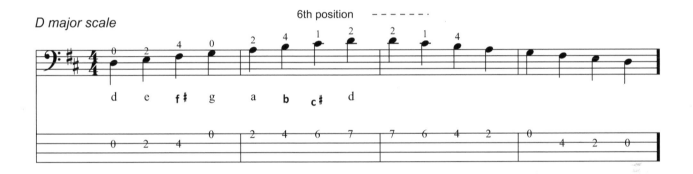

Every major scale contains the same interval order (1,1,1/2,1,1,1,1/2) they only differentiate in tone pitch.

Practise the scales until you feel familiar with them.

To play 'by ear'.

When you play in a band, you will get into the situation where you have to keep on playing although there is no sheet music available. What you could ask for, before the session starts is the 'key'. The key is very useful because most chord changes follow a specific pattern. In a piece played in D-major, the first and last note of the piece most likely a D. But which other notes will occur in the piece? Most likely the ones of the main harmony – tonic, subdominant and dominant (D,G,A).

Main harmony – tonic, subdominant, dominant.

The tonic can be found on the first scale degree of the diatonic scale, the dominant on the 5th and the subdominant on the 4th scale degree.

Key of C-major.

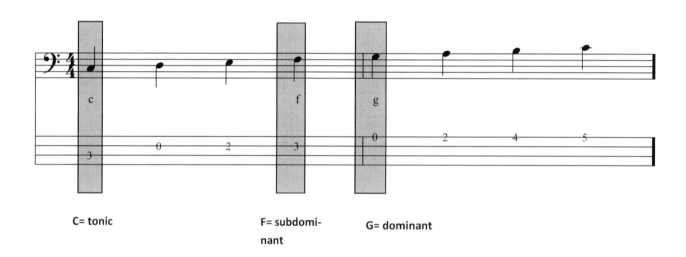

C= tonic   F= subdomi-   G= dominant
                  nant

Key of G-major.

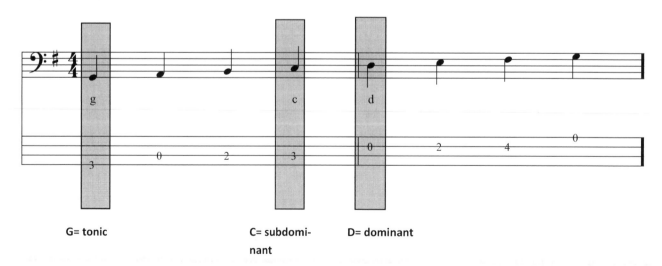

G= tonic   C= subdomi-   D= dominant
                  nant

Comping in practice.

In practice, the change between tonic, subdominant and dominant is slightly different. The interval between the tonic and the subdominant is a fourth, between the tonic and the dominant a fifth. These intervals are very easy to remember.

Ex 1:

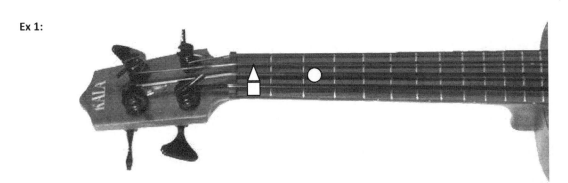

The three different symbols match the keynote (square=tonic), the fourth (triangle=subdominant) and fifth (circle=dominant). If you switch the starting point, these distances will always stay the same. To every note you play on your E-string you will find the fourth on the string below in the same fret and the fifth on the string below two frets up.Take a careful look at the examples.

If we pick a tonic (square!) on the second string (A-String), there are more possibilities:
Subdominant and dominant can also be played on the string above (E-String). The principle can be applied to every position played.

Ex 2:

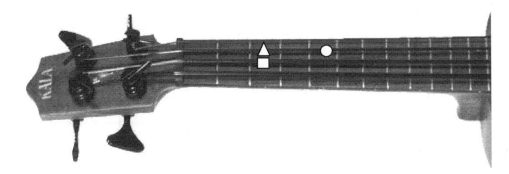

Ex 3:

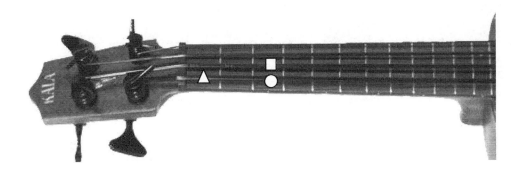

Comping with chord symbols.

As a bass player, you may have to play according to a sheet that only contains chord symbols. You can start by playing the key tone of the chord. Later on you can add further tones of the major or minor chord or chord extensions (6,7,9). To start playing the key tones, you have to acquire knowledge about the notes of your UBass. Below, you can find the notes of the first string, the E-string.

Notes on the E-String.

Track 16

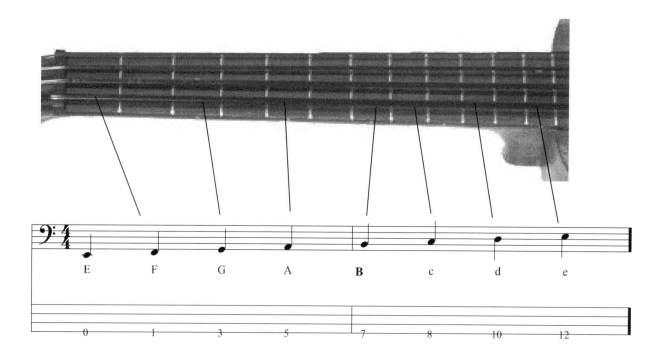

The octave.

To every note on your E-String, you can play the corresponding octave if you tap two frets up and two strings below. Exercise playing the octave by moving up the E-String upwards and tab the key note with your first and the octave with your third finger.

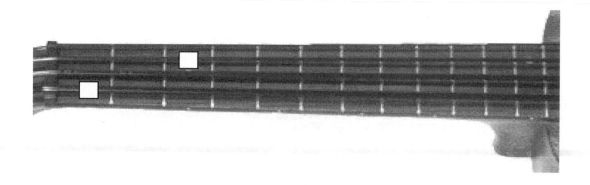

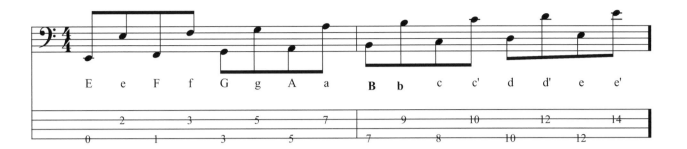

Key notes of the A-String.

Repeat the exercise on the A-String

Track 17

Just as explained before, find the octave two frets up on second string below.

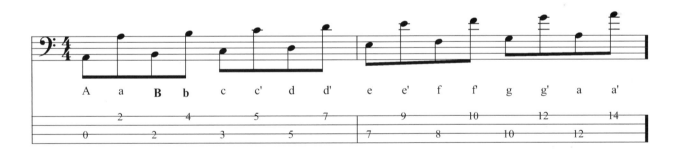

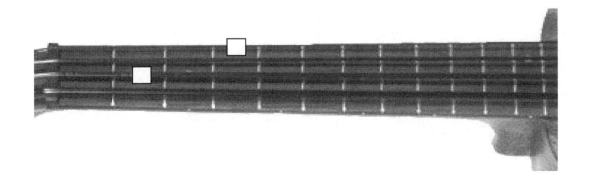

Overview.

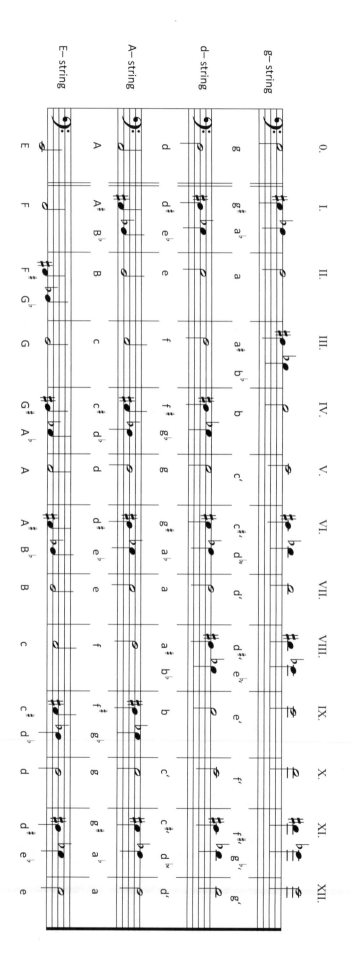

Common bass accompaniment patterns.

Below, you can find standard bass lines that fit the accompaniment of many songs. You can play fast eighth notes that sound a lot like rock music, or slow long-sounding notes depending on the tempo and style of your song. In addition, there is the typical 'latin' pattern that consists of a dotted quarter note followed by an eight note. To get a better knowledge how famous bass players do their job try to listen carefully to the bass lines of songs played in the radio. After a while, you will get a feeling for the style of bass line the song needs.

Track

18—22

1. Jazzy walking bass line

2. Latin bass line

3. Latin-Calypso

4. Fast dance tune

5. Rock

6. Pop Song

Track 23 –26

7. Rhumba

8. Boogie/ Rock'n Roll

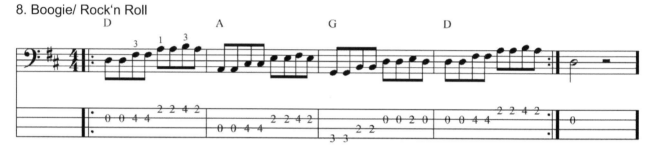

9. Latin

Chords.

The bass player most commonly plays single notes and avoids layering notes together. However, you can sometimes try to play chords on your UBass. Try to play the following exercise and keep the fingers of your left hand in place – the notes should layer together.

Track 27

(Barre—chord notation with music staff and tablature)

Special techniques.

Track 28

The slide.

Try out the slide technique. Just play one note and then move the finger of your left hand up or down the fret board without lifting it.

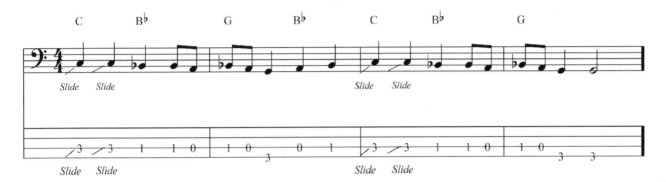

Hammer on, pull off (H.O., P.O.)

These techniques play an important role in rock and blues music. To play a 'hammer on', just tap the note, let it sound and then 'hammer' the next note 'on' your fret board – it should sound without the need to stroke the string again for the second note. The second note has to be tapped fast and sharply by bringing your fretting finger down on the fret board. The technique 'pull off' is just the opposite. The sound is not achieved by bringing the finger down on the fret board but by lifting it up. Tap a string and stroke it, whilst it vibrates 'pull' the tapping finger 'off' the fret board.

Track 29

Bassline with hammer on (H.O.)

Bass line with pull off (P.O.)

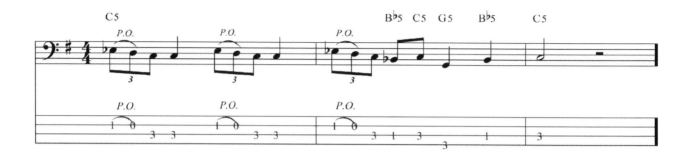

Ghost Notes.

Ghost notes are also called 'false' or 'dead' note, which have a great rythmical value without a pitch when played. These notes are great to add 'groove' to your bassline as you can see and hear clearly in our example on the DVD. The ghost notes are muted. This can be achieved in two different ways

1.   If you use a pick, you can mute the strings with the heel of your hand. Playing with a pick is ideal for this method of muting.

2. You can also mute the sound of the string with your left hand. Lift the picking finger slightly without losing touch with the tapped string.

Play the following exercise and use the muting methods.

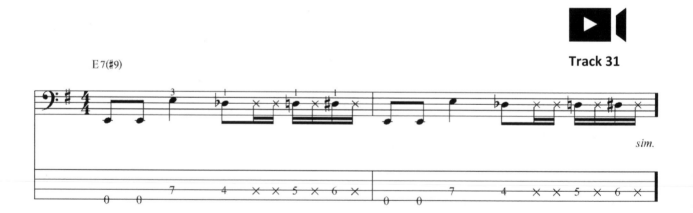

Play in a band.

As a bass player you obviously want to play in a band. Below, you can see several scores for bass, guitar and drum set (or cajon) that you can check out with your friends. If a drummer is not available, you can try 'body percussion', use your voice, hand, clapping, the table or simple rhythm instruments. Please note: the most important thing is to understand the 'division of business' between drummer and bass player!

Rock.

Track 32

Rock-Ballad.

Track 33

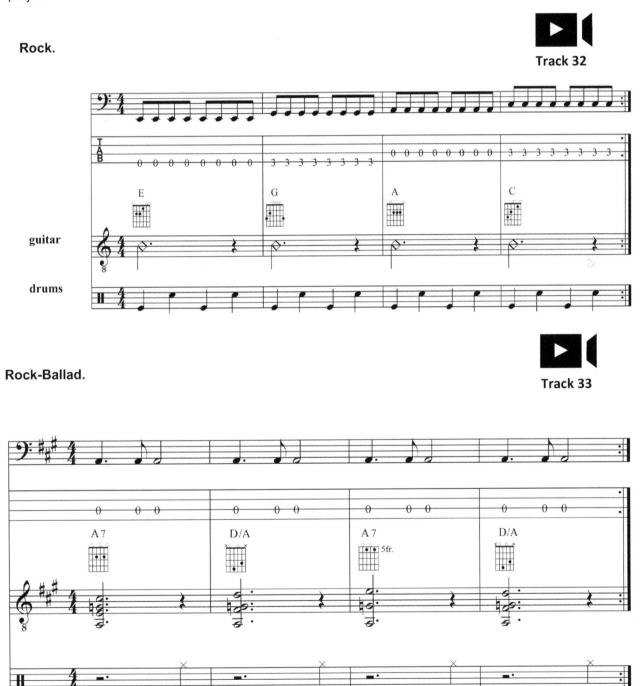

41

Boogie—Woogie.

Track 34

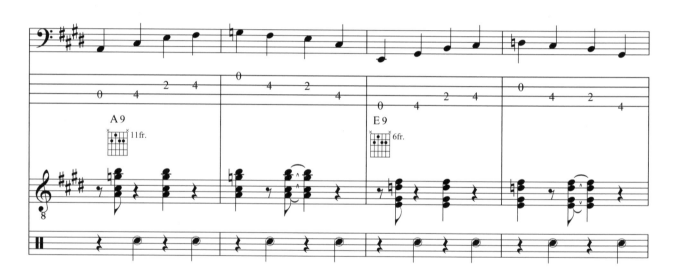

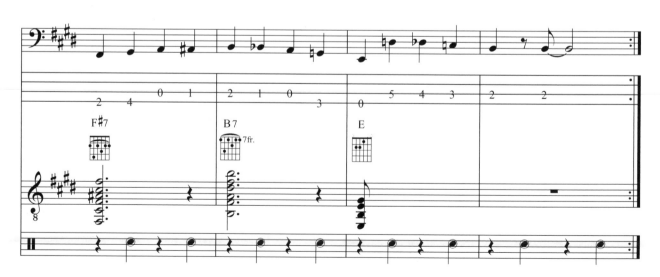

42

Blues-Rock.

Track 35

Rhythm'n Blues.

Track 36

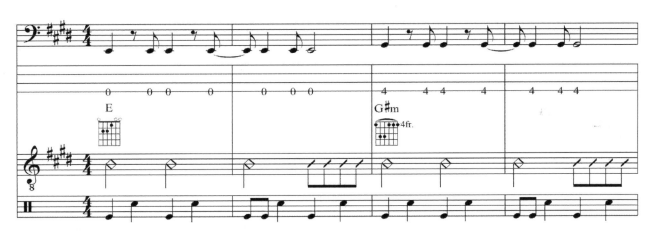

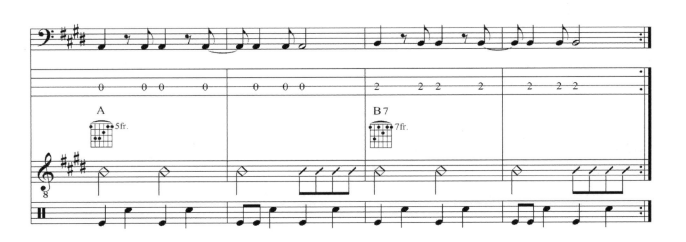

Latin.

Track 37

Rock'n Roll.

Track 38

Country.

Track 39

Solo pieces
for the bass ukulele.

Easy to intermediate level.

The Monkey

Track 40

Felix Schell

Sammy's Boogie

Track 41

Felix Schell

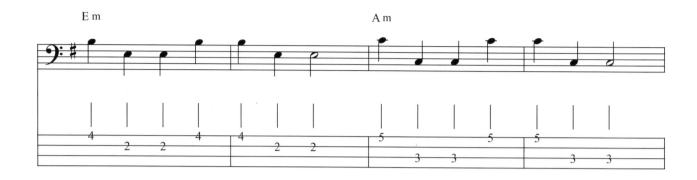

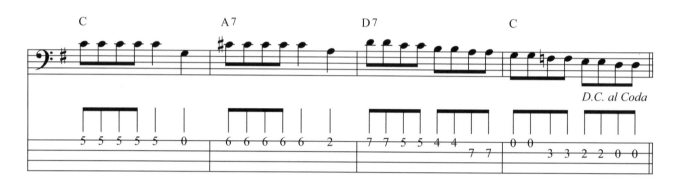

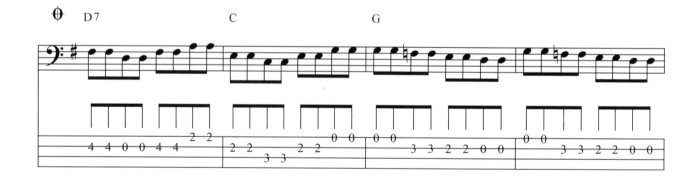

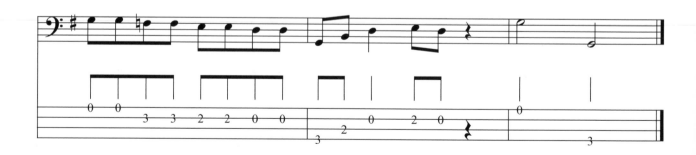

Walking With You

Track 42

Felix Schell

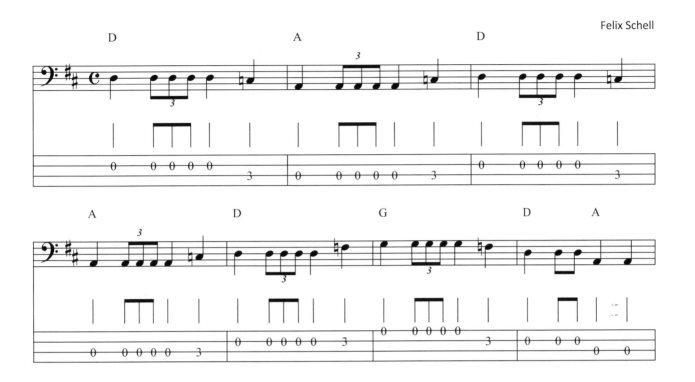

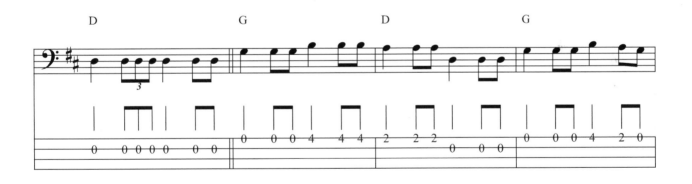

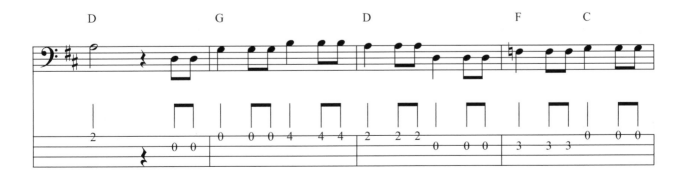

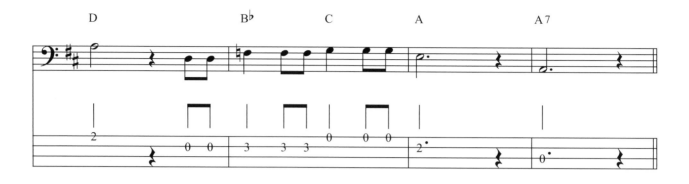

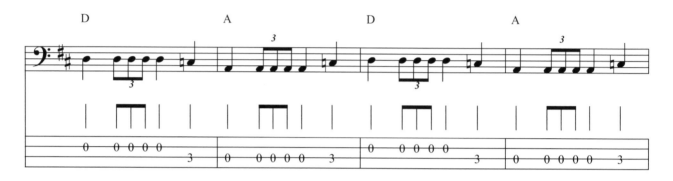

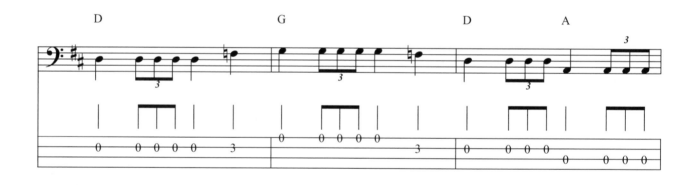

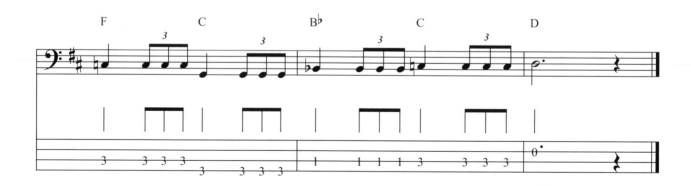

Voilà

Track 43

Felix Schell

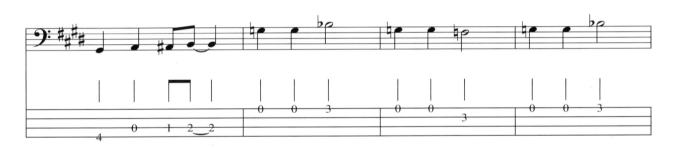

Calypso

Felix Schell

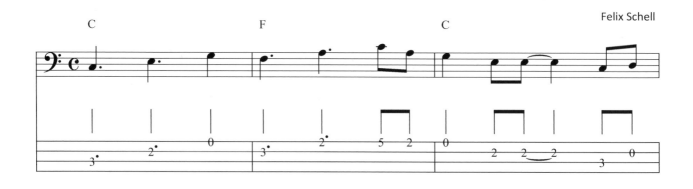

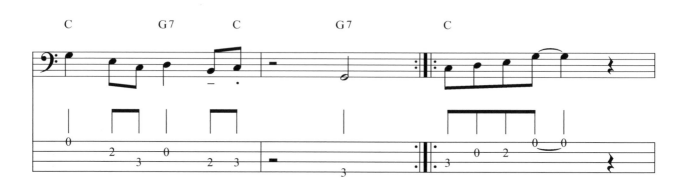

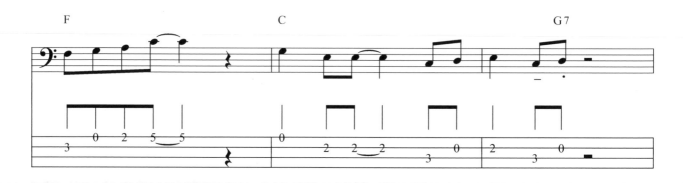

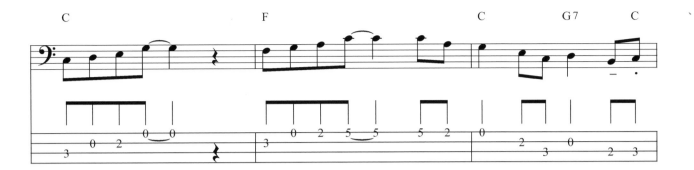

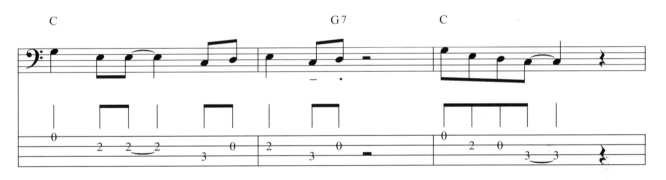

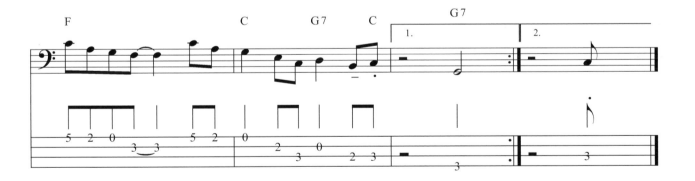

Duets for two UBasses

(in TAB)

Keep Cool, Man

Felix Schell

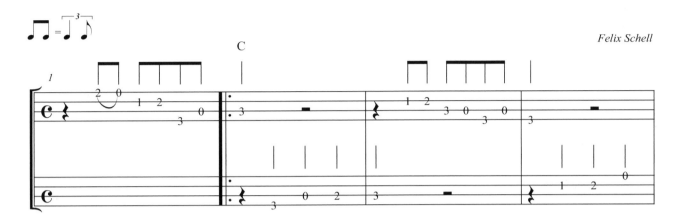

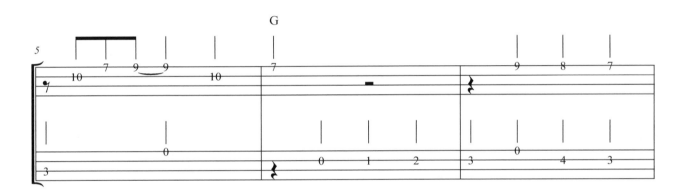

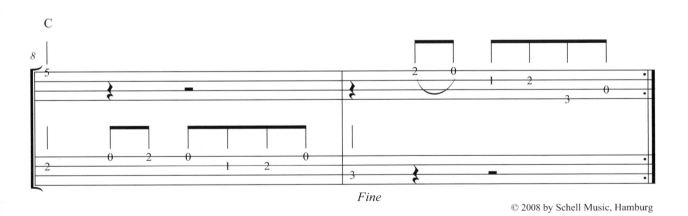

Fine

Blues for Paul

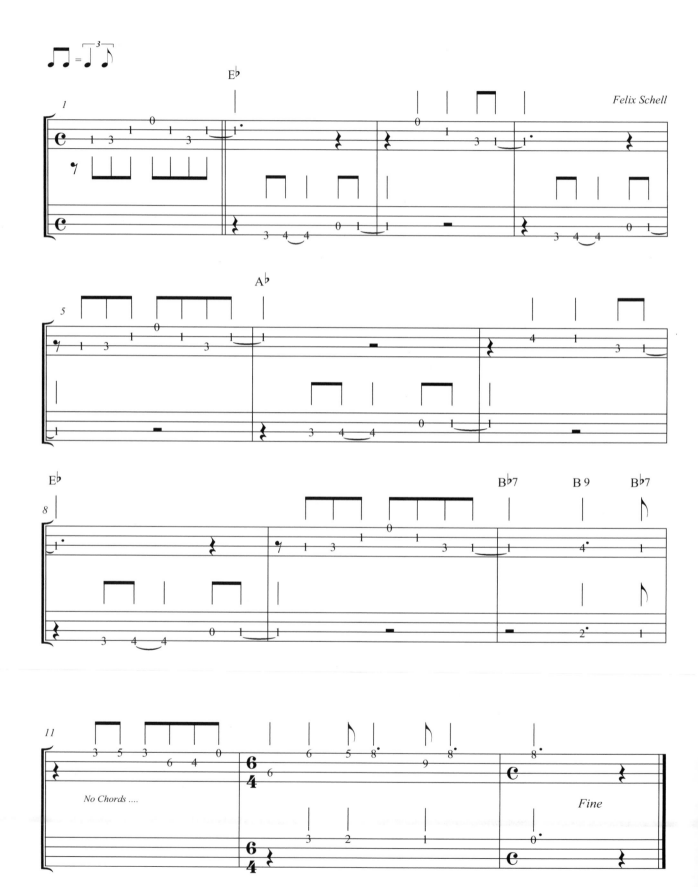

Songs

The following tunes contain a melody and a bass line. First try to play the melody on your UBass. Then try to sing. If that works, try to play the bass line while singing.

Old Mac Donald - G-major

Camptown Races - C-major

Clementine - E-major

Michael, Row the Boat Ashore - D-major

Old Mac Donald

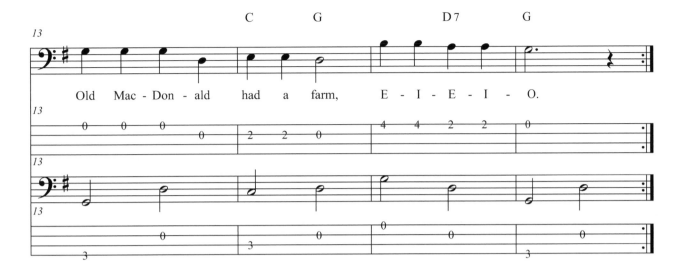

2. Old MacDonald had a farm, E-I-E-I-O.
   And on this farm he had some ducks, E-I-E-I-O.
   With a quack, quack here, and a quack, quack there.
   Here a quack, there a quack, everywhere a quack, quack.
   Old MacDonald had a farm, E-I-E-I-O.

3. Old MacDonald had a farm, E-I-E-I-O.
   And on this farm he had some dogs, E-I-E-I-O.
   With a woof, woof here, and a woof, woof there.
   Here a woof, there a woof, everywhere a woof, woof.
   Old MacDonald had a farm, E-I-E-I-O.

Camptown Races

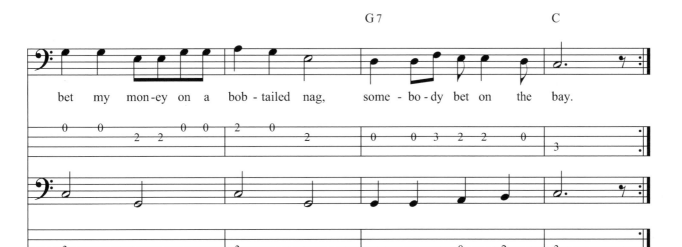

bet my mon-ey on a bob - tailed nag,   some - bo - dy bet on the bay.

2. The longtail filly and the big black horse, Doo-dah, doo-dah!
   They fly the track and they all cut across, Oh, doo-dah day!   *Chorus*

3. I went down South with my hat caved in, Doo-dah, doo-dah!
   I come back North with a pocket full of tin, Oh, doo-dah day!   *Chorus*

Clementine

American Folk Song

2. Light she was, and like a fairy,
   and her shoes were number nine,
   herring boxes without topses,
   sandals were for Clementine.

3. Drove she ducklings to the water
   every morning just at nine
   hit her foot against a splinter,
   fell into the foaming brine.

Michael, Row the Boat Ashore

2. Sister, help him trim the sail, alleluia.
   Sister, help him trim the sail, alleluia.

3. River Jordan's deep and wide, alleluia.
   River Jordan's deep and wide, alleluia.

4. River Jordan's chilly and cold, alleluia.
   River Jordan's chilly and cold, alleluia.

About.

Martin 'Bassmati' Schroeder.

Martin 'Bassmati' Schroeder (born 1980 in Hamburg) is living and working as a professional bass player, teacher and performer in Hamburg, Germany. At age 15 he attended lessons in multiple instruments, Guitar, piano and accordion. When friends founded the successful band 'Almost Amused' he discovered his love for the bass instrument. After his studies at the 'Hamburg School of Music', Martin toured as a bass player throughout Germany and parts of Europe. Since then, he participated in several Album and music video productions, joined TV and live concerts of well known band such as Pohlmann, No Angels, Sophie Ellis Bextor, Right Said Fred, Duncan Townsend and Graziella Schazad. Martin shares his knowledge about the bass in several Music schools and supports newcomer acts such as „Tom Klose" or „Constanze" (Producer Sven Waje – Fettes Brot, Nneka).

Liselotte Schell.

Liselotte Schell (born 1983 in Hamburg) started her music studies by playing guitar and piano. At the age of 16, she joined a school band. They already had a guitarist so she picked up the bass and stayed with it. She joined several bands in her free time and as her main job, Liselotte works as a lawyer, specialised in music, media and publishing law in Hamburg.

Made in the USA
Middletown, DE
04 June 2018